ARGENTINA * CHILE
PARAGUAY * URUGUAY

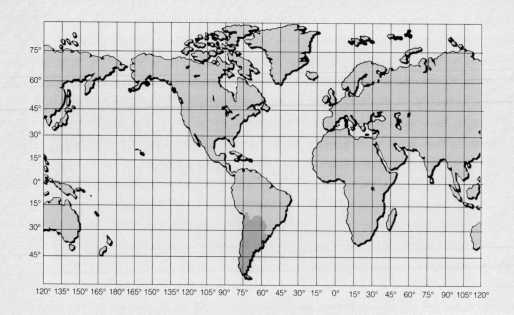

country	area (square miles)	population (1997)	capital	currency
ARGENTINA	1,068,380	34,800,000	Buenos Aires	peso
CHILE	292,280	14,200,000	Santiago	peso
PARAGUAY	157,060	4,900,000	Asunción	guaraní
URUGUAY	68,042	3,200,000	Montevideo	peso

ARGENTINA

CHILE

PARAGUAY

URUGUAY

ARGENTINA ✳ CHILE
PARAGUAY ✳ URUGUAY

Anna Selby

RSVP
**RAINTREE
STECK-VAUGHN**
P U B L I S H E R S
A Steck-Vaughn Company

Austin, Texas

Published by Raintree Steck-Vaughn Publishers,
an imprint of Steck-Vaughn Company

Design and typesetting Roger Kohn Designs
Commissioning editor Rosie Nixon
Editor Merle Thompson
Picture research Shelley Noronha
Maps János Márffy

We are grateful to the following for permission
to reproduce photographs:
Front cover: Robert Harding, *above* (L. Murray); Robert Harding, *below* (C. Bowman); Cephos, page 39 (R. & K. Muschenetz); Sylvia Corday, pages 10/11 (J. Smith); Eye Ubiquitous, pages 8, 41 *above left* (N. Wisciman); Robert Harding, pages 19 (C. Bowman), 28 (R. Frerck), 30 (R. Frerck), 42 (R. McLeod); Hutchinson Libraries, page 15 (M. Friend); Impact, pages 24 (C. Penn) 26 (H. Hughes); Roger Kohn, page 38 *below right*; Panos, pages 25 *above right* (C. Sattlberger), 32 (H. Hughes), 44 (Julio Etchart); Popperfoto, pages 27, 45 (G. Cameron, Reuters); Rex Features, pages 21 (P. Heim Sath), 22 (F. Arias), 31; South American Pictures, pages 12 (K. Jarvis), 14 (T. Morrison), 16 (T. Morrison), 17 (T. Morrison), 18 *below right* (R. Francis), 20 (T. Morrison), 29 (R. Francis), 33 (T. Morrison), 36 *above left* and *below right* (T. Morrison), 38 *above left* (P. Dixon), 40 (T. Morrison), 41 *below right* (T. Morrison), 43 *above left* (T. Morrison); Still Pictures, page 18 *above left* (Julio Etchart); Tony Stone, pages 13 (A. Smith), 34/35 (R. Van Der Hilst); Topham Picturepoint, pages 9, 25 *below*, 35; Trip, pages 23 (M. Barlow), 43 *below right* (E. Smith); WPL, page 37.

The statistics given in this book are the most up-to-date available
at the time of going to press.

Printed in Hong Kong by Wing King Tong

Library of Congress Cataloging-in-Publication Data
Selby, Anna.
Argentina, Chile, Paraguay, Uruguay / Anna Selby.
p.   cm. — (Country fact files)
Includes bibliographical references and index.
Summary: Provides information on the history, geography, society, industries, transportation, environment, and culture of Argentina, Chile, Paraguay, and Uruguay.
ISBN 0-8172-5408-0
1. Argentina — Juvenile literature.   2. Chile — Juvenile literature.
3. Paraguay — Juvenile literature.   4. Uruguay — Juvenile literature.
[1. Argentina.   2. Chile.   3. Paraguay.   4. Uruguay.]   I. Title.   II. Series.
F2808.2.S45   1999
980 — dc21   98-45225
CIP
AC

1 2 3 4 5 6 7 8 9 0 HK 02 01 00 99 98

C
O
N
T
E
N
T
S

Words that are explained in the glossary are printed in
SMALL CAPITALS the first time they are mentioned in the text.

INTRODUCTION

The four countries that form the southern part of the South American continent are very different from one another. These are the Republic of Paraguay, rural and LANDLOCKED; the tiny eastern Republic of Uruguay, the third smallest country in South America after French Guiana and Suriname; the vast, Europeanized Argentine Republic; and the long, narrow Republic of Chile, squeezed between the Andes Mountains and the Pacific Ocean. In total, these countries cover 1,586,223 square miles (4,108,000 sq km), which is almost half the land area of the United States. Their total populations amount to well over 55,000,000 people.

This is a land of great variety. The Andes Mountains run the entire length of the continent of South America. Some of the peaks rise to over 21,325 feet (6,500 m), and many have glaciers and snowfields. There are, however, some areas in the more northern parts where tropical climates and even deserts can be found.

Farming is vital to the economies of all four countries, and most of their exports are based on agricultural products. These vary widely from the cotton and timber of Paraguay to Argentina's huge exports of meat, sugar, and grains. Chile is alone among the four countries in having

▼ The 220-foot (67-m) high obelisk in the Plaza de la Republica is a familiar landmark in the center of Avenido 9 de Julio, in Argentina's capital, Buenos Aires.

important mineral resources. It is the world's leading producer of copper and a major supplier of precious metals.

In the past, however, the plentiful resources of these countries have not meant that their economies have been successful. This is because they have been undermined by unstable governments. The people have suffered military dictatorships, COUPS, revolutions, civil wars, and assassinations. Also, in 1982 Argentina went to war with the United Kingdom over the ownership of the Falkland Islands, or *Las Malvinas*, as they are called in Argentina. All of these problems have led to inflation and massive foreign debts. In recent years, however, the whole area has become more stable. The economies of each country have improved, and governments, for the most part, have become more liberal and democratic.

ARGENTINA, CHILE, PARAGUAY, AND URUGUAY AT A GLANCE

● Population density: Argentina has 31 people per square mile (12 per sq km); Chile has 47 (18); Uruguay 44 (17); and Paraguay 28 (11)

● Population capital cities: Buenos Aires, Argentina, 10,728,000; Santiago, Chile, 4,858,000; Asunción, Paraguay, 729,000; Montevideo, Uruguay, 1,248,000

● Highest peak: Mt. Aconcagua in Argentina, 22,835 feet (6,960 m).

● Major languages: Spanish is the main language of all four countries. However, 40% of Paraguayans speak Guaraní, and in Argentina, there is also some Guaraní spoken as well as Italian and Welsh.

● Major religions: Argentina, 93% Roman Catholic, 2% Protestant; Chile, 80% Roman Catholic, 6% Protestant; Paraguay, 96% Roman Catholic; Uruguay, 60% Roman Catholic, 3% Protestant, and 2% Jewish

● Major resources: copper ore, iron ore, limestone, precious metal ores, oil, hydro-electricity, timber, fish

● Major products: meat, wool, wine, cotton, oilseed

● Environmental problems: DEFORESTATION, water pollution

◀ *A typical Paraguayan farmhouse in Caaguazú, in rural eastern Paraguay*

THE LANDSCAPE

South America's landscape is one of extremes. For instance, Argentina is the eighth largest country in the world, and it is only slightly smaller than the entire Indian subcontinent. The enormous range of altitudes and latitudes means that there are endless variations in the region's landscape—from high plains to subtropical lowlands, from the flat PAMPAS to volcanic peaks and mountains, from tropical forest to glaciers, and from deserts to frozen fjords (narrow inlets). Chile and Argentina are divided by the huge mountain chain of the Andes, which runs from the north of Argentina to the south, before finally disappearing into the cold depths of the south Atlantic Ocean. The soaring volcanic peaks of the Andes tower over the high, arid Andean steppe, or ALTIPLANO, dotted with saline lakes called salares, all over 13,120 feet (4,000 m) high. East of the Andes, in northern Argentina, the lowlands alternate between open SAVANNAS and swampy lowland forests. Farther

PACIFIC OCEAN

ATACAMA DESERT

ANDES MOUNTAINS

Paraguay River

Paraná River

Uruguay River

Mt. Aconcagua
22,835 ft
(6,960 m)

Salado River

Plate River

PAMPAS

Colorado River

Negro River

PATAGONIA

Chubut River

ATLANTIC OCEAN

ARGENTINE LAKE DISTRICT

CHILEAN LAKE DISTRICT

N

0   500 km
0   300 mi

south, the pampas take over. This is an endless flat plain, now mostly farmland or cattle ranches. Below the pampas is the huge region of Patagonia, which has the same name both sides of the Andes, whether in Chile or Argentina. There are glaciers on the eastern, Argentinean side, but the most dramatic landscape is found on the Chilean side of the mountains— there are snow-capped volcanoes, impenetrably thick forests, and rocky, windswept, uninhabited islands. These form part of the Chilean fjords that extend all the way south to Cape Horn.

Central Chile consists of a series of fertile river basins known collectively as the Central Valley. Most of the population live

KEY FACTS

● Chile is more than ten times as long as it is wide.
● *Pampa* is a South American Indian word for "flat, featureless expanse of land."
● Tierra del Fuego, at the southernmost tip of South America, has a cold, bleak climate, but its name means "land of fire." It got its name because the fires lit by the original inhabitants of the island were spotted by the early European sailors on their voyages of discovery.
● Paraguay is bordered mostly by rivers, including the Paraná in the south and east and the Paraguay in the northwest.
● From its northernmost to its southernmost points, Argentina stretches as far as the distance from Scotland to the Sahara Desert.

in this area. Farther north is the Atacama Desert, one of the driest places on Earth.

Chile also has various groups of islands, or archipelagos, in the Pacific, including the famous Easter Island (Rapa Nui), which is 2,355 miles (3,790 km) from the coast. This is known throughout the world for its unique *moai*, or huge stone figures. All of these islands were produced by the action of underwater volcanoes. Easter Island's triangular shape was formed, for example, by the meeting of three separate lava flows. Volcanic activity and frequent

◀ *The pampas in Argentinean Patagonia. Most of the best pampas land has been enclosed for horse and cattle ranches or for crop cultivation.*

earthquakes are still commonplace, especially in the south of Chile. On occasion, coastal towns have been wiped out by tidal waves.

Although it is one of South America's smallest countries, Uruguay is still large when compared to most European countries. It is about the size of England and Wales or the state of North Dakota. It shares borders with both Brazil and Argentina

and has a scenic Atlantic Ocean coastline. Less fertile than the Argentinean pampas, the rolling hills on its northeastern border are very similar to those of southern Brazil. It is famed in South America for its beautiful beaches, as well as its dunes, headlands, and vast lagoons.

Paraguay is the northernmost of the four countries and borders Brazil, Bolivia, and Argentina. It has no coast, and the capital,

◄ *The Torres del Paine National Park, in Chilean Patagonia, has some of the most spectacular scenery in the world. Torres is the Spanish word for "towers" and describes the shape of these ice-capped mountains.*

▼ *The Iguazú Falls on the border of Argentina and Brazil are more than 1.2 miles (2 km) wide. Over 176,570 cubic feet (5,000 cubic m) of water make the 230-foot (70-m) drop every second.*

Asunción, is connected to the Atlantic Ocean only by the Paraguay and Paraná rivers. It is about the same size as the state of California. Half of the country is covered in forests, and much of it is subtropical. Compared to other South American countries, it lies quite low, rising only to 1,970 feet (600 m). In the west of the country is the Gran Chaco, a vast plain that stretches to the Bolivian border. This now consists mostly of huge ranches or ESTANCIAS. This area is almost deserted with only 4 percent of the population there.

CLIMATE AND WEATHER

Since Argentina, Chile, Paraguay, and Uruguay are all in the Southern Hemisphere, their summers occur during the months of November to March and their winters from May to September. However, because of the vast range of altitudes and latitudes within the area, the four countries all have very different climates. There are also very great variations within each individual country.

In Chile, for example, the Atacama Desert in the north has soaring daytime temperatures that, in the summer, average 95°F (35°C). It is so dry that no plant or animal life can exist. In the same area, however, the early mornings can be extremely cold before the fierce sun causes the temperatures to rise again. In total contrast, the south of the country has virtually continuous cold weather, with some of the stormiest conditions in the world. In Tierra del Fuego, the island at the southern tip of the continent that belongs partly to Chile and partly to Argentina, the winter average temperature is 40°F (4°C). Even in the summer, it rises only to 52°F (11°C). Around the capital of Santiago, however, there is mostly a pleasant Mediterranean climate.

Chile also has extremely high altitudes, and in the mountains there is snow for most of the year. In the winter, the passes leading to Argentina and Bolivia are frequently blocked. In fact, in the Chilean Andes there is enough snow for skiing for five months of the year—often while the coast is basking in the sun not much more than 93 miles (150 km) away. Because the

▼ *Cantegril Beach, Punta del Este, Uruguay, one of the country's popular sandy beaches.*

▶ *Many people go skiing in the winter at popular resorts in the Andes, such as Bariloche, in Argentina.*

mountains are so high, the ultraviolet rays of the sun can cause severe sunburn, and many people suffer from soroche, or altitude sickness.

Uruguay, by contrast, has one of the most agreeable and mild climates in the Southern Hemisphere. It is warm even in the winter, and frosts are very rare. The summers are quite dry by South American standards and reliably hot without the temperatures soaring to uncomfortable levels. Together with its beaches, this climate has made Uruguay a favorite vacation destination for South Americans from all over the continent.

KEY FACTS

● There are areas in northern Chile's Atacama Desert where no rainfall has ever been recorded.

● During the summer in Paraguay, it is very hot and humid. This is the time when most rain falls, and in Asunción there can be as much as .8 inches (2 cm) of rainfall a day.

● South of Buenos Aires, there are few ports in Argentina, because the tidal range along the Atlantic coast is so great that it is unsafe for shipping.

Western Paraguay, on the other hand, has a hot, humid climate all year-round, with summer temperatures averaging an uncomfortable 95°F (35°C). In the winter, the temperatures are mild, but sudden cold fronts, known as pamperos, sweep up from Argentina in the spring and autumn, causing temperatures to drop very suddenly—as much as 36°F (20°C) in just a few hours. The eastern part of the country has even higher summer temperatures of around 104°F (40°C), and the little rain evaporates quickly in the heat. The area's agriculture, therefore, has to depend on irrigation rather than rainfall.

Chile is a much wetter country than Argentina, because rain sweeping in from the Pacific Ocean to the west falls there

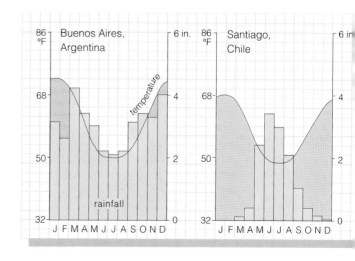

▲ **Although it has a very inhospitable climate, the Atacama Desert has been populated for a long time. Thousands of years ago, Andean Indians settled there along the coast to fish for their food.**

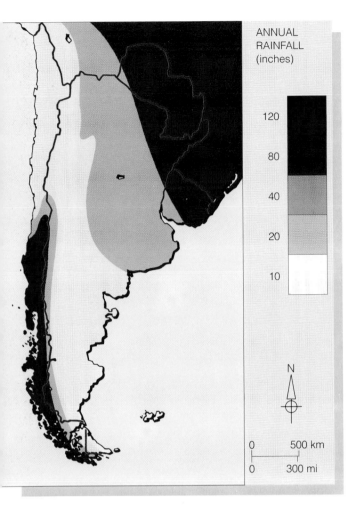

ANNUAL
RAINFALL
(inches)

120

80

40

20

10

N

0   500 km

0   300 mi

first as the rain clouds are forced to rise over the Andes. In the altiplano, or high plain, in the far north of Argentina, it is arid, and irrigation is needed for farming. However, in the summer, there can be sudden rainstorms with flash flooding and even snow. Rainfall increases steadily farther south, and on the pampas, south of Buenos Aires, the small rivers often flood. This problem is made worse by the almost uniformly flat terrain. Argentinean Patagonia is much drier than the Chilean side of the Andes, but in the extreme south there is sufficient snow to produce the largest glaciers in the Southern Hemisphere outside of Antarctica.

▶ *The Iguazú River flows through the lush rain forest of southern Brazil near its border with Argentina.*

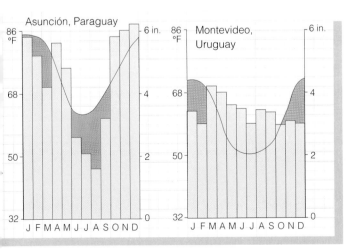

The mighty Itaipú Dam, a joint Brazilian-Paraguayan project that has enabled Paraguay to produce 99.8 percent of the electricity it needs.

to Chile, it has also made its economy dependent on the world prices for minerals. So when these prices dipped in the 1981 world recession, Chile went through a period of severe economic decline. The economy is now, however, generally much recovered.

Chile also has abundant reserves of oil, natural gas, and coal. Argentina, too, is self-sufficient in petroleum and other energy resources. However, Argentina, which is one of the wealthiest countries in Latin America, has failed to make the most of these. This is because the country has suffered from political upheavals and serious mismanagement of the economy.

Most of Chile's oil comes from the extreme south of the country. This oil drilling platform is at Punta Arenas, in the Strait of Magellan.

Although the name *Argentina* means "land of silver," only Chile out of these four countries has great mineral wealth. Chile produces huge amounts of copper and also has vast reserves of iron ore, manganese, lead, gold, silver, zinc, molybdenum, sulfur, and nitrates. It is the leading exporter of precious metal ores. In 1996 the world's total exports were valued at US$ 337,600,000. Chile exported US$ 61,700,000 worth of precious ores, compared to US$ 8,200,000 worth by the United States and US$ 35,000,000 worth by the entire European Union. However, while this natural wealth is very important

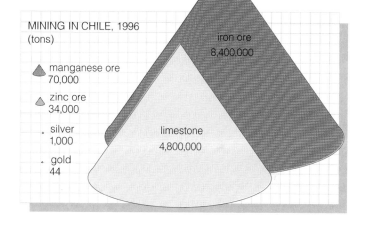

◀ The Chuquicamata copper mine is in the north of Chile in the Atacama Desert, and is built on a vast scale. It employs 9,000 people, and the ore is extracted from a pit 2.5 miles (4 km) long, 1.2 miles (2 km) wide, and 2,070 feet (630 m) deep. Every day, 60,000 tons of ore are processed.

MINING IN CHILE, 1996
(tons)

manganese ore
70,000

zinc ore
34,000

silver
1,000

gold
44

iron ore
8,400,000

limestone
4,800,000

Uruguay and Paraguay are both extremely poor in terms of mineral resources. Paraguay, however, has now begun to use its rivers to produce hydroelectric power. Since it is such a poor country,

KEY FACTS

● Today Chuquicamata is a huge, modern copper mine, but copper has been mined there since very early times, even before the INCAS arrived.
● Although the Itaipú Dam has given Paraguay great benefits in energy resources, it has caused an environmental disaster. By creating a reservoir of 520 square miles (1,350 sq km), 656 feet (200 m) deep, it has produced an area of stagnant water that has provided anopheles mosquitos with a new breeding ground. This has brought malaria back to an area from which it had virtually disappeared.
● In 1995 Chile produced 2.56 million tons of copper ore, over a quarter of the world's total production.

it has needed the help of its neighbors to do this. The Itaipú Dam, which harnessed the potential of the mighty Paraná River, is the world's largest hydroelectric project, with a capacity of 12.6 million kilowatts. The whole venture cost US$ 25 billion and was financed by Brazil. The result is that Paraguay now generates almost all of its electricity from water power and has some left over to export to Brazil. However, the project has left Paraguay with an increased foreign debt because of maintenance costs and repayments for its share of the capital.

POPULATION

South America is a very sparsely populated region compared to much of the rest of the world. This is partly because some areas are uninhabitable due to their climate or geographical position. However, it is also because the waves of immigration over the centuries have never been continuous. The population, once settled, has generally grown very slowly.

The descendants of the original native people, in most cases, make up only a very small portion of the population. When the first CONQUISTADORES arrived in the 16th century, the native peoples had been isolated from the diseases of the rest of the world for at least 10,000 years. Consequently, in much of the region, the arrival of Europeans reduced the local population by up to 95 percent. This was due not so much to mistreatment but to deadly contact with smallpox, influenza, typhus, and other diseases to which they had no resistance.

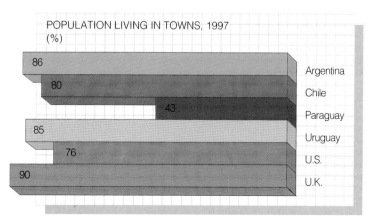

POPULATION LIVING IN TOWNS, 1997
(%)

86	Argentina
80	Chile
43	Paraguay
85	Uruguay
76	U.S.
90	U.K.

◀ *Calle Florida, part of Buenos Aires' busy shopping area, reflects the city's European flavor.*

There are now small groups of pure descendants from the original inhabitants living all over the region. However, the size of their communities is insignificant when compared to the number of European or mestizo people— those of mixed European and Indian ancestry. In Argentina, the country's INDIGENOUS POPULATION numbers 100,000, but this includes several different groups, including the Quechua and the Mapuche. Argentina had a policy of promoting

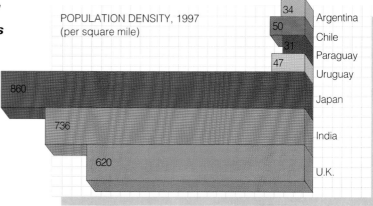

POPULATION DENSITY, 1997
(per square mile)

34	Argentina
50	Chile
31	Paraguay
47	Uruguay
860	Japan
736	India
620	U.K.

European immigration in the 19th century and modeling itself after Europe. The new settlers quickly displaced the Indians. Not all of them were of Spanish origin, and many came from Italy, Wales, England, Germany, the Ukraine, and the Basque

▶ *President Carlos Menem of Argentina is of Syrian descent. He is the most prominent of a small group of immigrants from the Middle East to have gained political influence. Although he is now a Roman Catholic—a necessary requirement for presidency—he was originally a Muslim.*

POPULATION

region. Some of these immigrants to Argentina have preserved something of their culture. This is particularly true of the Welsh in the Chubut province, where, until recently, Welsh was the second language and appeared on signposts alongside the Spanish. Buenos Aires also has a large Jewish community, and there has been an influx of immigrants from the Middle East, including the country's president, Carlos Menem. Most people in Argentina live in cities. This is also true of Chile and Uruguay, although Paraguay has a much more rural population.

In Paraguay, less than half the population live in towns, and the capital, Asunción, has only 729,000 inhabitants. Unlike Argentina, where the Indian

▼ *A Chilean band with traditional instruments. They are playing in the street to celebrate a FIESTA marking an eclipse of the sun.*

KEY FACTS

● There have been so many Italian immigrants to Argentina that there are now more Italian surnames in the Buenos Aires area than Spanish ones.
● Buenos Aires has the eighth largest Jewish community in the world (400,000), but it has been the focus of terrorist bombing. There were explosions in the Israeli Embassy in 1992 and a Jewish cultural center in 1994, when many people were killed.
● Uruguay is South America's smallest Spanish-speaking country.
● The Mapuche of Chile were famed as silversmiths long before the arrival of the conquistadores, and they continue to make their exquisite artifacts today.
● For a long time, the inhabitants of Easter Island were thought to be of South American origin. It is now accepted that they are Polynesian and are related to the Maori of New Zealand and the islanders of the Pacific, such as the Tahitians and Tongans.

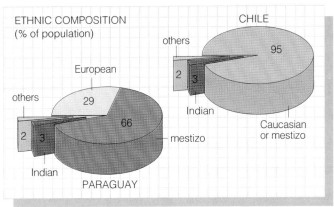

ETHNIC COMPOSITION
(% of population)

CHILE

others
2   3
95
Indian
Caucasian
or mestizo

European
others   29
2   3   66
mestizo
Indian
PARAGUAY

▲ *Guaraní Indians in Asunción,*
Paraguay, selling local handicrafts.

as Spanish. There is a small population
(about 3 percent) of pure Indians, mostly
living in the Chaco region. Some, until very
recently, followed their traditional way of
life of hunting and gathering.

Although Uruguay's agriculture is vital
to its economy, the vast majority of the
population live in cities, nearly half of them
in the capital, Montevideo. The original
people, the Charruas, have almost died out,
although there is a tiny mestizo population
close to the Brazilian border. Most
Uruguayans are of European descent,
mainly Italian and Spanish. There is also

population declined and the Europeans took
over, in Paraguay the original inhabitants,
the Guaraní, integrated with the Spanish
settlers. As a result, the population is
now 66 percent mestizo, and the entire
population, including upper-class
Europeans, speaks Guaraní as well

a small population of people of mixed African and Uruguayan blood. These are descended from slaves brought to the country in the 19th century.

There are only a few people of full-blooded European ancestry in Chile. The great majority of Chileans are of mixed Spanish and Indian extraction (mestizo). Within this mix, people regard themselves as "mostly European" or "mostly Indian," but there is less racial diversity than in most South American countries. A small population of Africans led to the formation of another racial group, the mulattos. They have mixed black and European ancestors, while zambos are of black and Indian blood. Unlike Argentina, which absorbed

▲ In the mid-19th century, there was a large influx of Welsh farmers who settled in Patagonia. They have retained their cultural identity for more than a hundred years, as can be seen in this Welsh tea party.

many groups of immigrants from Europe during the 19th century, Chile had very few. Those who did come included Germans, French, Italians, and Yugoslavs. There is still a small Indian population including the Mapuche, the Aymara, and the Rapa Nui of Easter Island.

DAILY LIFE

The long history of political and financial upheavals has left many South Americans feeling uncertain about basic things in their day-to-day lives that people from other countries take for granted. Argentina, for example, suffered from runaway inflation that, at its worst, was over 3,000 percent. At this rate, the price of a loaf of bread increased by 8 percent every day. During the worst days of political repression, many political prisoners were taken away and never heard from again. Now, however, all four countries appear to be more stable, both in terms of political freedom and in their economies. Because of this, people are able to live with greater certainty about the future than they have for decades.

▼ *The vast sheep and cattle estancias of Argentina are run by gauchos, the cowboys of South America.*

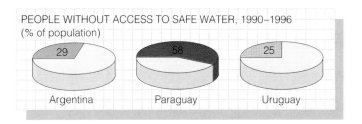

PEOPLE WITHOUT ACCESS TO SAFE WATER, 1990–1996
(% of population)

Argentina	Paraguay	Uruguay
29	58	25

▼ *Gauchos barbecue meat on an open fire as they journey with their animals to fresh pastures.*

HEALTH

Standards of health care vary throughout South America. Argentina has a good public health-care system, while in Uruguay cash payment is often necessary before the sick are allowed into a hospital. There are a number of diseases that are still quite common in South America that have been wiped out in more developed countries. These include typhoid, polio, cholera, and, in some areas, malaria.

One of the main health problems is a lack of clean drinking water. In major cities, the water is often—but not always—safe to drink, but in the countryside it is often contaminated. Also, food may not be

▲ *A polo match in Buenos Aires. Polo is the national game of Argentina.*

▶ *Soccer player Diego Maradona becomes a national hero when Argentina wins the World Cup in Mexico City, in 1986.*

prepared hygienically either in the towns or in the countryside, so dysentery is widespread.

RELIGION

All four countries are predominantly Roman Catholic, the religion brought by the conquistadores. However, the official religion is often filled with local superstitions, depending on the region. In rural Paraguay, for instance, many people are said to regard their local parish priest as a healer or even a magician. There are many religious festivals in South America, often celebrated with processions, music, and feasting. People often dress in special costumes and carry religious statues through the streets.

In Chile, Evangelical Protestantism has grown rapidly. The largest new church is the Pentecostal Methodist Church. Evangelical Protestantism has also gained ground in Argentina, where television evangelists are popular. Roman Catholicism is still the state religion,

KEY FACTS

● In Paraguay children between the ages of 10 and 14 make up almost 8% of the workforce.
● South America not only produces a great deal of the world's wine, but they drink a lot of it, too. Argentina, Chile, and Uruguay are all in the world's top twenty countries of wine drinkers.
● Argentineans have many television stations to choose from. There are 32 private stations, 10 state ones, and 2 run by universities.
● Chile produces beautiful jewelry using silver and lapis lazuli, a bright blue stone that is found only there and in Afghanistan.

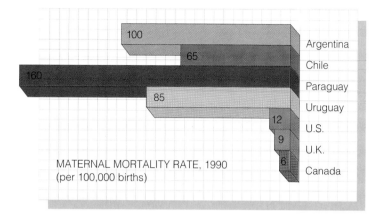

MATERNAL MORTALITY RATE, 1990
(per 100,000 births)

100	Argentina
65	Chile
160	Paraguay
85	Uruguay
12	U.S.
9	U.K.
6	Canada

is also a good public secondary school system that follows the French model, in which all subjects are compulsory. Higher education in universities and teacher training colleges is also free. Argentina's literacy rate of 94 percent is one of the highest in South America.

In Chile, 90 percent of the adults can read and write. Elementary education is free for at least eight years. There is both public and private secondary education, although many children leave school early to work and help support the family. In Uruguay, primary education is also free and compulsory. Enrollment in the free secondary schools is also high, but not mandatory. In Paraguay, school is required

nonetheless, and President Menem had to convert from Islam before he was able to become leader. However, the Roman Catholic Church received a great deal of criticism in the 1970s and 1980s when it was supportive of the military government, which was infamous for its torture and murder practices.

EDUCATION

In Argentina, education is free and compulsory from ages 5 to 12. There

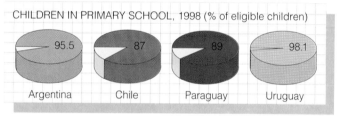

CHILDREN IN PRIMARY SCHOOL, 1998 (% of eligible children)

Argentina	Chile	Paraguay	Uruguay
95.5	87	89	98.1

◄ **The tango is the national dance of Argentina. In the 1930s, when it first became popular, people would often tango in the streets. This demonstration took place at San Telmo, the Sunday Antiques market in Buenos Aires.**

◄ *South Americans often celebrate religious and secular holidays with processions and pageants. This is the Fiesta de Cuasimodo procession in Chile's capital, Santiago.*

until age 12. It has one of the lowest literacy rates in South America at 81 percent.

LEISURE

In many ways Argentina has a very Europeanized culture. The spectacular Teatro Colón in Buenos Aires (named after Christopher Columbus, whose name in Spanish is Colón) opened in 1908 as one of the foremost opera houses in the world. In musical terms, however, Argentina is probably best known for its national dance, the tango, still the most commonly heard music in the country. In Chile the most famous dance is the Cueca, in which handkerchiefs are waved to the accompaniment of guitar, harp, and handclapping.

South America is also famous for its writers, notably Jorge Luis Borges and Manuel Puig of Argentina, the Chilean poet Pablo Neruda, the Paraguayan poet and novelist Augusto Roa Bastos, and Juan Carlos Onetti, the Uruguayan novelist.

FESTIVALS AND HOLIDAYS IN CHILE	
January 1	NEW YEAR'S DAY
March/April	EASTER
May 1	LABOR DAY
May 21	NAVY DAY
August 15	THE ASSUMPTION
September 18–19	INDEPENDENCE DAYS
October 12	DISCOVERY OF AMERICA
November 1	ALL SAINTS' DAY
December 8	THE IMMACULATE CONCEPTION
December 25	CHRISTMAS DAY

Theater is popular in all four countries, and Argentina has a flourishing film industry.

Sports are very popular throughout the region, particularly soccer, at which South Americans excel. Argentina is famous for its world-class polo teams and its polo ponies. The ponies are renowned for their speed and ability to change direction at the slightest touch from their riders. It has also produced many world-class sports personalities, such as the tennis player Gabriela Sabatini and race car driver Juan Manuel Fangio, who won the World Grand Prix Championship five times in the 1950s.

RULES AND LAWS

At some time in the last few decades, all South American countries have experienced political repression and upheavals on a grand scale. Military dictatorships, coups, revolutions, and civil wars have all meant very real danger in the lives of ordinary people. Books could be censored and removed, and there was no freedom of expression. Even large family gatherings, such as birthday parties, could be regarded with suspicion and require police approval before they could take place. People who ignored any of these rules would be imprisoned and often "disappear." In Argentina, during the JUNTA, or military dictatorship of the 1970s and early 1980s, there were officially 9,000 cases of such disappearances. In these instances, people were tortured, illegally imprisoned, and eventually murdered. However, unofficial estimates are three times this number.

Even before this, however, Argentina had been at the mercy of corrupt, unjust, or ineffectual governments for many years. The country's most famous rulers were undoubtedly the Peróns. Juan Carlos was the president, but his wife, Eva, better

▼ **Los madres de los desaparecidos—*or "the mothers of the disappeared"—in Buenos Aires. They march in front of the presidential palace in memory of their children who were murdered in the 1970s and early 1980s.***

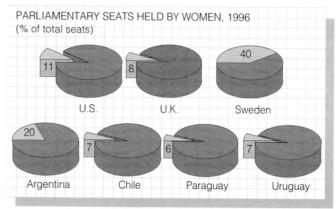

◀ *Eva Perón first came to politics as the wife of President Juan Perón, but her charismatic public speaking soon gave her a special role in Argentinean politics. Her death in 1952 traumatized the entire country.*

PARLIAMENTARY SEATS HELD BY WOMEN, 1996
(% of total seats)

11 — U.S.
8 — U.K.
40 — Sweden
20 — Argentina
7 — Chile
6 — Paraguay
7 — Uruguay

known as "Evita," had just as much popular support. While Perón was elected by democratic vote, he then went on to change the constitution. He abolished the clause prohibiting the reelection of a president, and in 1952 he was elected for a second 6-year term. He was, however, unable to control galloping inflation, and the country slipped further and further into debt to foreign nations. His regime collapsed in 1955. A series of short-lived presidents and military juntas followed until the military took over in 1966. They held power until 1973, when the country was torn by riots, and Perón returned briefly as president. He died the following year, and his regime, led by his second wife, was overthrown by the military junta in 1976.

This junta was to collapse because of the 1982 war with Great Britain over the Falkland Islands, known in Argentina as Las Malvinas. While this war had great national support initially, it collapsed after

KEY FACTS

● One of the most distinguished South American politicians was Uruguay's José Batlle y Ordóñez. In the first two decades of the 20th century, he organized the first welfare state in the continent, including pensions, unemployment benefits, and limits on the length of the working day.

● Eva Perón was an actress before she married the president. Women were given the vote in 1947 because of her influence. Today Argentina has one of the best records in the world for the number of women in politics, with a high percentage of women in parliamentary seats.

● Chile won its independence from Spain in the early 19th century under the command of an Irish-Chilean named Bernardo O'Higgins. He became the head of the first Chilean government. There is a street in Santiago named after him— Avenida Bernardo O'Higgins.

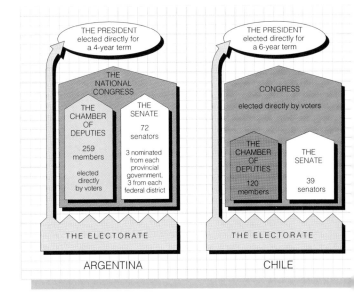

▲ **The death of President Allende of Chile in 1973 is remembered every year. This commemorative procession took place in 1990.**

only 74 days, and the junta soon followed. The country returned to civilian rule first with President Raúl Alfonsín and then with President Carlos Menem. Argentina now has a constitution and democratic elections, and the influence of the army, while still great, is gradually ebbing.

Chile's most famous president was the socialist Salvador Allende, elected in 1970 in the country's first democratically elected government. His reforms nationalized banking, insurance, communications, and industry, but this led to hostility from Chile's business community and the United States. In 1973 his government was overthrown in a CIA-backed military coup. Allende, according to varying reports, either committed suicide or was murdered. General Augusto Pinochet took over and banned all political activity in a brutally repressive regime. This came as a great shock to Chile, which is traditionally a

 *Alfredo Stroessner was president of Paraguay from 1954 to 1989 in one of the longest and most corrupt dictatorships in South America.*

peaceful country. Thousands of Allende's supporters were arrested, tortured, and executed. All political parties and trade unions were banned. Free elections finally took place again in 1989, although General Pinochet remained army commander until 1998. Since then, there has been a feeling of liberation throughout the country.

Uruguay started the 20th century with what was a pioneering welfare state

compared to the rest of South America. However, by the mid-1960s, economic problems had caused severe political unrest. This eventually led to a military takeover in 1973. Until 1985, torture became routine, and the regime was accused of appalling human rights abuses, with more than 60,000 people detained. Julio María Sanguinetti was elected in 1984, with the military suppressing the other political parties. But since that time, there has been a gradual loosening of military power.

Paraguay suffered perhaps the worst regime in all of South America under General Alfredo Stroessner, who ruled the country in 1954 for 35 years. This brutal government had a complete disregard for human rights and permitted no real political opposition. When Stroessner was finally overthrown in 1989, there was a movement to destroy the thousands of monuments built in his honor. In 1992 a constitution was established, although it is still uncertain whether democracy will last.

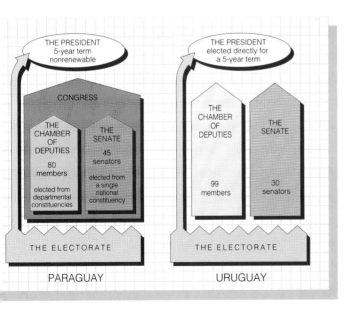

THE PRESIDENT
5-year term
nonrenewable

CONGRESS

THE CHAMBER OF DEPUTIES
80 members
elected from departmental constituencies

THE SENATE
45 senators
elected from a single national constituency

THE ELECTORATE

PARAGUAY

THE PRESIDENT
elected directly for a 5-year term

THE CHAMBER OF DEPUTIES
99 members

THE SENATE
30 senators

THE ELECTORATE

URUGUAY

FOOD AND FARMING

South America, in general, and Argentina, in particular, produce vast quantities of food and products from livestock. Argentina's economy relies heavily on agriculture. It is one of the world's biggest meat and wool producers from the livestock on its huge estancias, which run beef cattle in the north of the country and sheep in the south. Less well known is the fact that Argentina is also the ninth largest producer of cotton in the world and grows vast quantities of oilseeds, such as soybeans, sunflower seeds, cottonseeds, groundnuts, and grape seeds. Argentina, in fact, produces a total of 19 million tons of oil from these crops every year, making it the fifth largest producer in the world. The Argentinean farming industry also exports huge quantities of wheat, wine, corn, sugar, fruits, and vegetables, in addition to growing these for the home market.

Chile is less dependent on agriculture than Argentina. Chile traditionally grows such crops as cereals, seeds, vegetables, and fruits. However, its long Pacific coastline has made fishing an important industry with an annual catch as large as the entire catch of the United States and the U.K. put together. This includes

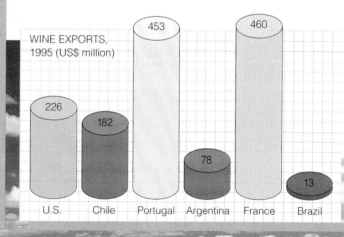

LAND USE

- farmland
- fruit trees, vineyards, and plantations
- permanent pasture
- woods and forest
- rough grazing
- nonproductive land

N

0   500 km
0   300 mi

WINE EXPORTS, 1995 (US$ million)

U.S.	Chile	Portugal	Argentina	France	Brazil
226	182	453	78	460	13

▼ *Talcahuano has the best harbor in Chile. It is an important fishing port and the main naval center in the country.*

KEY FACTS

● Argentina is the fifth largest wool producer and the tenth largest meat producer in the world.
● Chile has a coastline of 3,320 miles (5,338 km) and exclusive fishing rights over 617,810 sq mi (1,600,000 sq km).
● Uruguay's meat processing was pioneered on the coast at Fray Bentos, known worldwide for its corned beef.
● Prepared meats are a vital part of the South American economy. Argentina exports US$ 381 million-worth of prepared meats. This is just behind the world leader, the United States, with US$ 389 million.

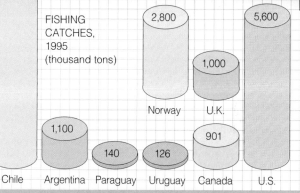

FISHING CATCHES, 1995 (thousand tons)

Chile	Argentina	Paraguay	Uruguay	Canada	U.S.	Norway	U.K.
7,600	1,100	140	126	901	5,600	2,800	1,000

◀ *Sheep farming is the main industry of Patagonian Argentina, and its huge estancias cover thousands of square miles.*

220 species of edible fish. Chile also has a large wine-making industry. The first vineyard was established by the Spanish in 1551, in order to supply wine for the religious celebration of the mass. Because of its natural frontiers of ocean, mountains, and desert, Chile is one of the few countries in the world not to have been affected by the PHYLLOXERA epidemic, which has wiped out vineyards in other countries.

Farming accounts for 25 percent of the GROSS DOMESTIC PRODUCT of Paraguay and employs 45 percent of its workforce.

Much of this is subsistence farming, with families working small areas of land to feed themselves and selling the little that is left over at local markets. It does export beef, corn, sugar, timber, and cotton, but, due to its landlocked position in the middle of the continent, transport costs are high, making its products very expensive.

Uruguay's main industry is farming and, in particular, pastoral farming with cattle and sheep estancias occupying more than three-quarters of the land. Only 10 percent of the land is devoted to growing crops, although much more could be cultivated. Nevertheless, cereals, including rice, make an important contribution to the economy. A wide range of fruits and vegetables is also grown.

One of South America's unique crops is yerba maté, also known as Paraguayan tea. It is grown and drunk throughout the region, but it is particularly popular in Argentina. Maté is made from the leaves of a hollylike plant, and Argentineans drink about four times as much of it as they do coffee.

CATTLE, 1994 (million head)	
Chile	3
Paraguay	8
Uruguay	10
U.K.	11
France	20
Russia	48
Argentina	50
U.S.	100

▲ **In the low Chaco of Paraguay, sugarcane is transported by ox-drawn cart, or carreta, to a local market.**

► **In the old sector of Montevideo, a greengrocer sets out an appetizing array of fruits and vegetables.**

TRADE AND INDUSTRY

Agricultural products, such as foods, oils, leather, wool, and cotton play a large part in all South American economies, although this is less true in Chile, where mining and fishing are also as important. In Argentina, there is a huge industry based on meat processing, while about 80 percent of the country's cereal crops are exported. Other industries have advanced rapidly since the country's oil reserves have been exploited. These include the manufacture of paper, steel, cars, textiles, and chemicals.

Chile's economy is based principally on the mining of copper, iron ore, gold, and silver. Timber and paper are exported in sizeable quantities. For this reason, cultivated forests are taking up more and more areas of the country, although native forests have been declining proportionately. Although agriculture is an important industry in Chile, it does not produce enough food for the country. Great quantities of foodstuffs are, therefore, imported. Manufacturing industries include food processing, metalworking, and textiles.

In Paraguay, wood products, cotton, and

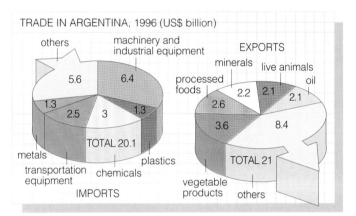

TRADE IN ARGENTINA, 1996 (US$ billion)

IMPORTS
others 5.6
machinery and industrial equipment 6.4
metals 1.3
transportation equipment 2.5
chemicals 3
plastics 1.3
TOTAL 20.1

EXPORTS
minerals 2.2
live animals 2.1
oil 2.1
processed foods 2.6
3.6
8.4
vegetable products
others
TOTAL 21

KEY FACTS

● In the last decade, privatization of nationalized industries has been widespread throughout the region. Argentina, in particular, has sold off much of the state sector, including the state telephone and oil companies.

● Uruguay is still one of the most state-dominated countries in the region and is renowned for its difficult bureaucracy.

● Argentina's industrial output is substantial. It stands at about US$ 85 billion a year.

◀ *The beef industry is vital to Argentina's economy. This vast cattle market on the outskirts of Buenos Aires stretches as far as the eye can see.*

NUMBER OF VISITORS, 1996 (thousands)		
61,000		France
25,000		U.K.
9,700		Greece
4,100		Australia
3,600		Egypt
4,200		Argentina
1,500		Chile
300		Paraguay
2,000		Uruguay

◀ *Tourism is becoming more and more important to the economies of South America. Because of its wide variety of climates and landscapes, the choices are unlimited. They range from warm, sunny beaches to the glaciers of Antarctica (left).*

cigarettes form the principal industries besides agriculture, while the hydroelectric plants it has built produce a surplus of energy for export to its neighbors. However, Paraguay has suffered because of its landlocked geographical position. This makes its exports very expensive to transport and, therefore, uncompetitive in the world market. Paraguayan workers, in both farming and industry, are very poorly paid, and much of the economy is boosted by CONTRABAND, including the trade of illegal drugs.

The Uruguayan economy is essentially based on agriculture, with beef as its chief export. Industries include oil refining and the manufacture of cement and textiles, all based around Montevideo. Tourism is particularly important to Uruguay, with many visitors from other Latin American countries. Tourism, in fact, is growing throughout South America and already accounts for about 20 percent of Argentina's income. Many visitors come from the United States and

▲ *Beautiful silver objects have been produced in Chile and Argentina for a very long time.*

Europe, as well as from other Latin American countries.

FOREIGN DEBT

In spite of Argentina's high industrial output, it still has one of the highest international

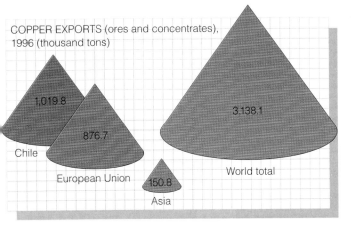

COPPER EXPORTS (ores and concentrates), 1996 (thousand tons)

1,019.8 Chile

876.7 European Union

3,138.1 World total

150.8 Asia

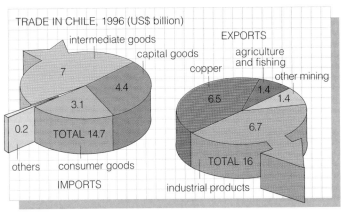

TRADE IN CHILE, 1996 (US$ billion)

IMPORTS
- intermediate goods 7
- capital goods 4.4
- 3.1
- 0.2 others
- consumer goods
- TOTAL 14.7

EXPORTS
- agriculture and fishing
- copper 6.5
- other mining 1.4
- 1.4
- 6.7 industrial products
- TOTAL 16

foreign debt, any significant economic development is hampered.

MERCOSUR

In 1995 Mercosur was established, creating a common market within the South American nations of Brazil, Argentina, Uruguay, and Paraguay. It is based on establishing a free-trade zone to encourage commerce and industry and reduce overall prices. However, there is no free movement of labor allowed among the countries, so young people in Uruguay and Paraguay have become illegal workers in neighboring countries. This deprives their own countries of many of their best workers. In 1996 Chile became an associate member of Mercosur.

debts in the world. The problems of debt and inflation have plagued all of the South American economies for decades. Inflation is still very high in Uruguay, Paraguay, and Chile, although Argentina has brought it slightly more under control in recent years. However, with such a high portion of the countries' incomes spent on servicing

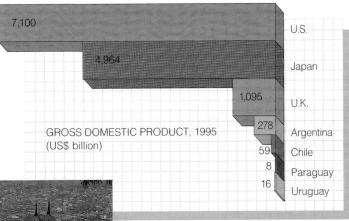

GROSS DOMESTIC PRODUCT, 1995 (US$ billion)

- 7,100 U.S.
- 4,964 Japan
- 1,095 U.K.
- 278 Argentina
- 59 Chile
- 8 Paraguay
- 16 Uruguay

◀ *Valparaiso was founded in 1542 and grew to become the principal port in Chile. After the opening of the Panama Canal in 1914, its position declined. It is still an important fishing and naval port, but its historical buildings have virtually disappeared because this area has suffered repeated earthquakes.*

TRANSPORTATION

The Andes, running down the entire length of South America, more or less divide the land into two parts. Access overland from east to west is limited and at times hazardous. Many of the passes through the mountains between Argentina and Chile become blocked in the winter because of snow. In the summer, however, buses travel through the high passes between these countries and also across the borders of Argentina with Brazil, Bolivia, Uruguay, and Paraguay, and from Chile to Bolivia and Peru. In the south of the continent, particularly in Chile, boats are an important means of communication.

Argentina has the best transportation system in the region. This includes an extensive domestic air service and a railroad network that is the seventh largest in the world. The railroad was originally built by the British and has many stations that resemble those of English country towns. There is a similarly extensive road network, covering 134,220 miles (216,000 km), nearly all of it hard surfaced. Argentina has one of the highest per capita (per head) car-ownership rates in South America. It also has one of the worst driving records. After 2,000 traffic deaths during only two months in 1995, the problem became known as *la guerra del transito*—"the traffic war."

Chile's mountainous terrain, with the Atacama Desert in the north and the fjords and off-shore islands of the south,

KEY FACTS

● Argentina has 21,250 miles (34,200 km) of railroad network.
● Traffic accidents are the main cause of death for Argentineans between the ages of 5 and 35.
● Asunción, Paraguay, has an extensive streetcar (vehicle on rails) network as well as bus routes.

◀ *Paraguay's tiny rail network uses antiquated, wood-burning steam locomotives.*

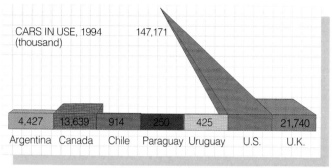

CARS IN USE, 1994 (thousand)						
4,427	13,639	914	250	425	147,171	21,740
Argentina	Canada	Chile	Paraguay	Uruguay	U.S.	U.K.

and no passenger trains, although there are freight trains. The roads in the interior of the country are rough and unpaved, and only a few cars travel on them. The most common way of crossing to Argentina is by ferry or hydrofoil from Montevideo, and there are also roads across the borders with Brazil and Argentina.

Paraguay has three border crossings to Argentina, two to Brazil, and one to Bolivia. Only 10 percent of Paraguay's roads are paved, however, and car ownership is low. In the countryside, horses and oxcarts are still important forms of transportation.

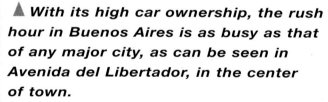

▲ *With its high car ownership, the rush hour in Buenos Aires is as busy as that of any major city, as can be seen in Avenida del Libertador, in the center of town.*

▼ *In Encarnación, Paraguay's third largest city, the horse and cart is still a common form of transportation.*

has made it difficult to develop a good internal transportation system. Coastal boat services were the main form of transportation from one town to the next within Chile until the early 20th century. This is still true in the south. However, there is now an established road network, not all of which is paved, and most Chileans travel by bus or car. Santiago has a good underground railroad system and good air links with the rest of the country.

Uruguay has limited domestic air services

THE ENVIRONMENT

South America, with its vast empty spaces, small population, low industrial output, and low car ownership, has little atmospheric pollution when compared to the United States or Europe. However, there are few environmental controls either, and most Latin American governments show little interest in introducing any. One of the main problems is deforestation. In spite of its tiny size, Paraguay is tenth in the world league of deforesters. A great deal of the country is forested, but much of the native forest is being replaced by cultivated forest for the timber trade. Between 1980 and 1993, more than 36 percent of Paraguay's natural forests were destroyed. There are a few national parks and nature preserves in the country, but many animals are in danger of extinction. Among them are the giant anteater, the giant armadillo, the jaguar, and the pampas deer.

Argentina now has an extensive system

▲ The Lauca National Park in the north of Chile stretches to the frontier with Bolivia and features numerous snowy volcanoes, ten of which are over 19,685 feet (6,000 m) high.

of national parks, where a large number of endangered species are protected. These include the Andean condor, the Argentinean boa constrictor, and a great variety of whales around its shores. However, there have also been some major environmental problems in Argentina. These include industrial pollution near Buenos Aires, dumping of nuclear waste, deforestation, and overgrazing in Patagonia.

Chile also has an extensive system of national parks and preserves where native species are protected. The vicuña, a species of llama, was hunted almost to extinction. By 1970 there were only 400 left in the country, but since becoming a

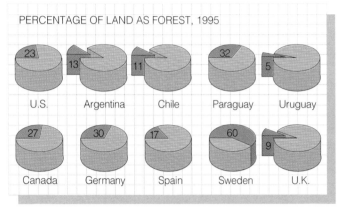

KEY FACTS

● In the mid-1970s, the Chacoan peccary was rediscovered in Paraguay. For over 50 years, scientists had believed it was extinct.

● Paraguay has 365 species of birds, including 21 parrots.

● The llama, alpaca, guanaco, and vicuña are all camelids—South American camels.

● Volcanoes are still active in Chile. In 1994 El Laima erupted for the first time in 37 years and spewed ash, lava, and smoke all over the Andean lake district. Although three-quarters of a million people live there, no one was killed.

PERCENTAGE OF LAND AS FOREST, 1995

U.S.	Argentina	Chile	Paraguay	Uruguay
23	13	11	32	5

Canada	Germany	Spain	Sweden	U.K.
27	30	17	60	9

protected species, numbers have grown to 12,000. Although no native birds migrate north to the United States, many fly south from North America to spend the summer in the Southern Hemisphere. None of the tropical birds of South America are in Chile, because it has the wrong terrain for them. Instead, the Chilean pigeon and the mockingbird live in the central area, while in Patagonia, there are the steamer duck, the Humboldt penguin, the Magellanic penguin, the Inca tern, and the storm petrel.

▲ *The jaguar was once common in the savannas of Chile, but because of hunting it is now an endangered species.*

▶ *While part of Argentinean Tierra del Fuego is a national park, there is substantial logging in other parts. This has led to the destruction of entire forests.*

THE FUTURE

In recent years, there has been political progress throughout South America. Democracy has returned in some form to most of the countries, and human rights are gradually improving. The long-term economic problems, however, have not been so easy to solve. In Uruguay, for instance, HYPERINFLATION resulted in the introduction of two new currencies in the course of 20 years. In 1996 Uruguay's inflation was running at over 40 percent and Paraguay's about 45 percent, although these figures are low compared to those from just a few years earlier.

At the root of these problems is a combination of government corruption, mismanagement, and the immense foreign debt South America faces. Because these debts are so massive, huge sums of money are needed to service them

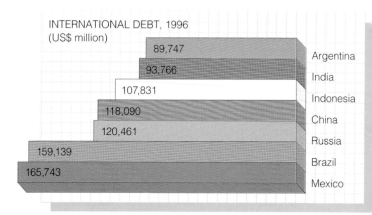

INTERNATIONAL DEBT, 1996
(US$ million)

89,747	Argentina
93,766	India
107,831	Indonesia
118,090	China
120,461	Russia
159,139	Brazil
165,743	Mexico

(to pay off the interest so that the sum originally borrowed does not grow any bigger). The interest payments run at an average of 40 percent of the entire export earnings of these countries. When added to capital repayments, this rises to 60 percent of all foreign earnings. In effect, it is impossible to repay the debts, and they simply get bigger every year. In the long

▲ *U.S. President Bill Clinton congratulates Chilean President Eduardo Frei for his opening speech at the second Summit of the Americas, on April 18, 1998. One of the main issues discussed was free trade.*

◀ *A new shopping mall in Montevideo, Uruguay, has been built on the site of a former high security prison where many political prisoners were once detained.*

term, Latin America's only real hope is for agreement to be reached among the world's richer nations to cancel out third-world debt.

The economic problems are made worse by the fact that, because of the instability of their countries, South Americans take their money out of their own countries and invest it abroad. Since the profits from economic success are not put back in, new industry is not generated. Thus, the

gap between poor and wealthy widens.

Despite all these problems, South America has many advantages. It is a land that is rich in natural resources, with a vibrant and optimistic people. It is hopeful that, in the future, Argentina, Chile, Paraguay, and Uruguay will be able to develop their very great potential.

KEY FACTS

● The Yacyreta Dam in Paraguay—the largest in the world—started production of hydroelectric power in 1994. At peak capacity, it can produce 2,700 megawatts of electricity. This equals the output of three average-sized nuclear power plants.
● Uruguay has signed trade agreements with China and Russia in an attempt to avoid economic dependence on its giant neighbors, Argentina and Brazil.

FURTHER INFORMATION

- **ARGENTINA EMBASSY**
1600 New Hampshire Avenue, NW
Washington, D.C. 20009

- **EMBASSY OF CHILE**
1732 Massachusetts Avenue, NW
Washington, D.C. 20036

- **EMBASSY OF PARAGUAY**
2400 Massachusetts Avenue, NW
Washington, D.C. 20008

- **EMBASSY OF URUGUAY**
2715 M Street, NW, 3rd Floor
Washington, D.C. 20007

BOOKS ABOUT THE REGION

Dwyer, Christopher. *Chile*. Chelsea House, 1997.

Kent, Deborah. *Buenos Aires*. Children's Press, 1998.

Liebowitz, Sol. *Argentina*. Chelsea House, 1998.

GLOSSARY

ALTIPLANO
A Spanish word meaning "high plain." It is used to describe the expanse of high level land in the Andes region.

CONQUISTADORES
The Spanish conquerors of South America who arrived in the 16th century.

CONTRABAND
Illegal trade.

COUPS
Violent or illegal changes in government.

DEFORESTATION
The clearance of trees in order to use the land for a different purpose.

ESTANCIAS
Vast ranches for raising sheep or cattle.

FIESTA
The Spanish word for "party" or "celebration."

GROSS DOMESTIC PRODUCT
The total value of all the goods and services produced by a country in a year, except for money earned from investments abroad.

HYPERINFLATION
Extreme inflation that occurs when the currency drops in value so rapidly over a period of time that prices can rise on a daily basis.

INCAS
Indians who originally came from the area around Cuzco in Peru. By the 15th century, they had built a huge empire in South America, which stretched up to the borders of Colombia and Ecuador and covered much of Chile and Bolivia.

INDIGENOUS POPULATION
The original inhabitants of a particular region.

JUNTA
A military dictatorship.

LANDLOCKED
A country or area that has no coastline. Landlocked countries are highly dependent on their neighbors to reach coastal ports, which are important for trade and industry.

PAMPAS
Flat, grassy plains.

PHYLLOXERA
An insect pest that lives on the roots of the grapevine and kills it. In the 1870s it destroyed nearly all European vineyards. The roots of the native American vine are immune to this pest.

SAVANNAS
Tropical and subtropical vegetation consisting of grasses, shrubs, and scattered trees. It is typically dry for most of the year but bursts into life when the first rains arrive.

INDEX